D0622518

Look What Came From France

by
Miles Harvey

Franklin Watts

A Division of Grolier Publishing

New York London Hong Kong Sydney

Danbury, Connecticut

Series Concept: Shari Joffe
Design: Steve Marton

Library of Congress Cataloging-in-Publication Data

Harvey, Miles.
   Look What Came From France / by Miles Harvey.
     p. cm. — (Look what came from)
   Includes bibliographical references and index.
   ISBN 0-531-11501-1 (lib. bdg.)   0-531-15964-7 (pbk.)
   1. France—Civilization—Juvenile literature.
   2. Civilization—French influences—Juvenile literature.
   I. Title.   II. Series.
   DC33.9.H37   1999
   944—dc21   98-36173
                                                              CIP
                                                               AC

Visit Franklin Watts on the Internet at:
http://publishing.grolier.com

Contents

Greetings from France!

When people think of the United States, the first thing that often comes to their minds is the Statue of Liberty. This famous statue is located on an island near New York City. It celebrates the American Revolution. But guess what? The Statue of Liberty was not made in the United States. It was made in France, a country located across the Atlantic Ocean on the continent of Europe. The statue was a gift from the people of France to the people of the United States.

France is not a very big land. In fact, it is smaller than the state of Texas. But it is famous for its food, fashion, books, art, and music.

The Statue of Liberty is not the only cool thing that came from France. In fact, many of the foods we eat, the clothes we wear, and the tools we use were invented in that amazing country. So come on! Let's take a look at all the great things that come from France!

French paper money and coins

The French flag

Inventions

Does your home or school have **wallpaper?**

The French came up with this idea about 500 years ago.

Many other cool inventions have also come from France. About 200 years ago, a man named André-Jacques Garnerin created the first **parachute.**

Early French wallpaper

He tested it by jumping out of a hot-air balloon high in the sky. Many people were shocked that he landed safely.

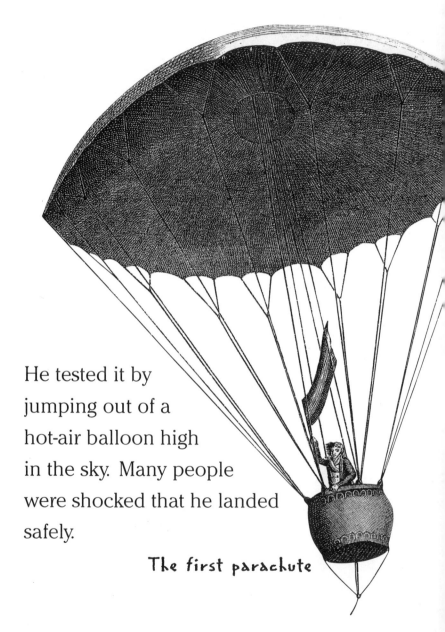

The first parachute

In 1816, a French man named René Laënnec came up with the idea of the **stethoscope.** This tool allows doctors to listen to people's heartbeats.

The first stethoscope

Louis Braille

Book written in braille

Person reading braille

In 1824, a man from France created a special kind of writing that allows blind people to read. It uses groups of raised dots that stand for letters of the alphabet. This amazing invention is called **braille.** Its creator, Louis Braille, was only 15 years old when he came up with the idea!

7

more inventions

Louis Pasteur

In 1864, a French scientist named Louis Pasteur figured out a way to make milk last for a long time before it spoiled. His idea is still used today. It is called **pasteurization.**

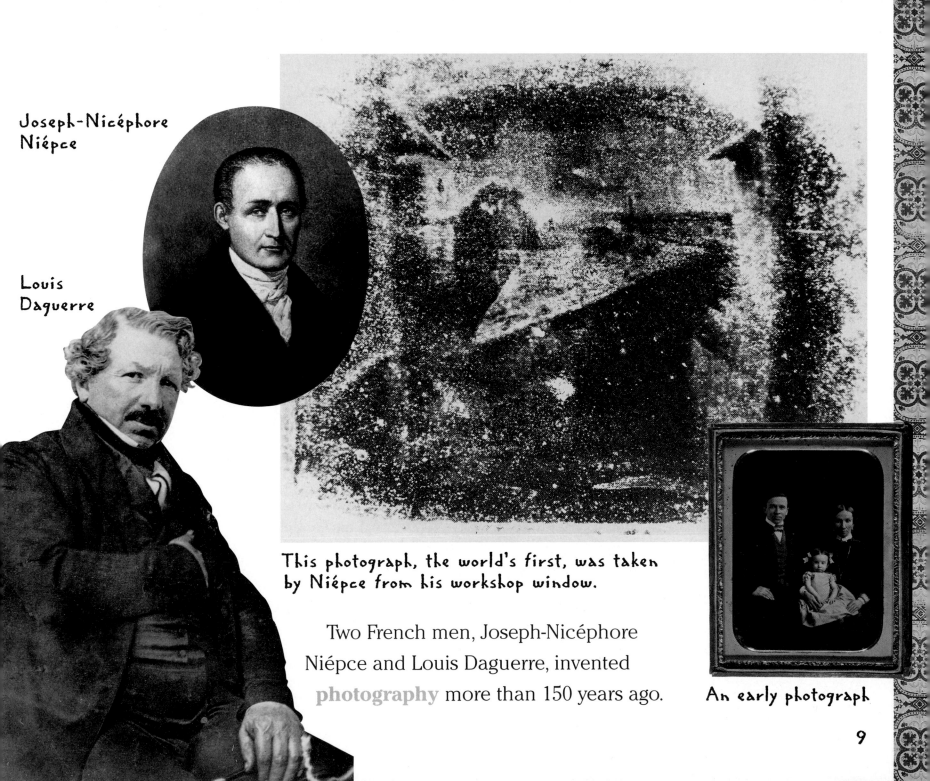

Joseph-Nicéphore Niépce

Louis Daguerre

This photograph, the world's first, was taken by Niépce from his workshop window.

Two French men, Joseph-Nicéphore Niépce and Louis Daguerre, invented **photography** more than 150 years ago.

An early photograph

A scene from an early sound movie produced by Leon Gaumont

About 100 years ago, a man from France named Leon Gaumont figured out a way to make sound movies. But it took many years for his invention to get popular. Until then, all movies were silent!

In 1942, two men, Émile Gagnon and Jacques Cousteau, invented a special kind of equipment that allows people to swim underwater for a long time. This invention is called **scuba gear.**

Jacques Cousteau (left) invented scuba gear.

11

Food

Crepes

French people really love to eat cheese. Some of the famous types of cheese that come from France are **Brie** and **Camembert.**

French people also enjoy **crepes,** pancakes that are rolled up and filled with different types of yummy food.

Camembert

Brie

French toast

Another tasty French dish is the soufflé, a puffy dish made of eggs and other ingredients.

Cheese soufflé

Many other famous kinds of food also come from France. One food that you've probably eaten is French toast. Another is a buttery, flaky roll called a croissant. Croissant is the French word for "crescent." Croissants got their name because they are crescent shaped, just like the moon!

Croissant

Kitchen Stuff

Take a look around your kitchen at home. Many of the things you'll see there originally came from France. For example, people in France came

Cork bottle top

up with the idea of the **cork bottle top** more than 450 years ago. Today, many bottle tops are made of plastic or metal.

The French invented the **coffee pot** about 200 years ago. In 1954, they also

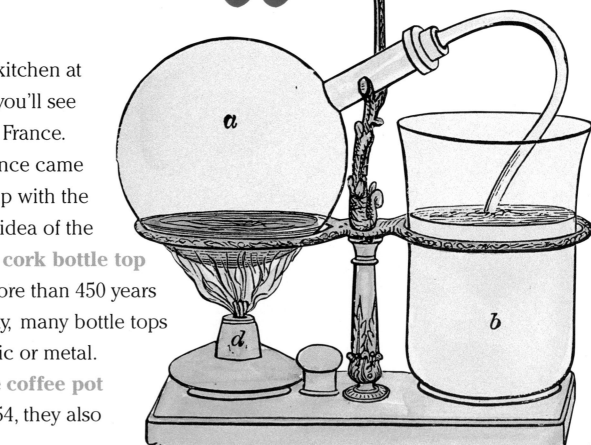

Drawing of the first coffee pot

14

Teflon pan

Today, food processors (left) can do the work that hand choppers (right) used to do.

came up with the idea of the Teflon frying pan. Teflon is a special material that is very easy to clean because food doesn't stick to it.

Another important cooking tool is the food processor, which was invented in France about 30 years ago.

Sunbeam
oskar jr.
CHOPPER PLUS

Transportation

An early bus

Look out at the street. The French came up with the original ideas for many vehicles that you may see. For example, more than 300 years ago, some people in the French city of Paris came up with the basic idea for a **bus.** And about 200 years ago, a French doctor invented the **ambulance.**

Both the bus and the ambulance were driven by horses. But also around 200 years ago, a French man named Nicolas Cugnot invented the first road vehicle to move under its own power. His invention was called the **steam carriage.** When he tried to drive it, it crashed into a wall and overturned. Still, some people think it was the world's first car!

An early ambulance

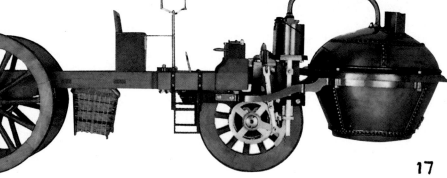

The first steam carriage

more transportation

Launch of the first hot-air balloon

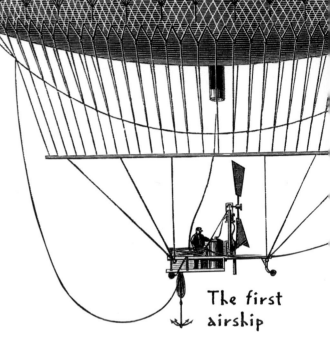

The first airship

Now look up at the sky. Several kinds of air travel were also invented in France. For example, Joseph and Etienne Montgolfier launched the first **hot-air balloon** more than 200 years ago. It was the first time people had ever been able to fly!

A hot-air balloon is hard to control. That's because it will go only where the wind takes it.

So in 1852, a French inventor came up with a way of attaching a motor to a balloon. He had invented the first airship. It wasn't a plane, but it was close!

People in France didn't come up with the idea for the airplane, but they did invent the first seaplane. A seaplane is a kind of aircraft that lands on water instead of on a runway. It was invented in 1910 by a French pilot named Henri Fabre. The French also helped create the world's fastest passenger airplane. It is called the Concorde jet, and it was invented in 1976 by people from France and England.

The first seaplane

Concorde jet

The Arts

No one knows exactly who invented **painting.** But the oldest paintings in the world are found on the walls of a cave in France. They are more than 30,000 years old!

An ancient cave painting in France

The French came up with the idea for **ballet** more than 400 years ago. Today, this popular kind of dance is performed in theaters around the world.

Scene from a modern-day ballet in France

French horn

French ballet dancers in the early 1800s

The **French horn** was invented in France about 400 years ago. Today, musicians all over the world use this marvelous instrument.

21

Games

About 500 years ago, people in France invented the kind of **playing cards** we use today. These cards are divided into four suits: spades, hearts, diamonds, and clubs.

Early playing cards

Europeans playing cards in the 1400s

Around the same time, the French invented **tennis.** Back then, the game was played only by the king of France and his best friends.

French students playing tennis in the 1600s

Holidays

Nineteenth-century drawing of a man having an April Fool's joke played on him

On April 1, some people celebrate April Fool's Day by playing practical jokes on each other. Many people believe this holiday began in France nearly 450 years ago.

Another French holiday takes place on July 14. It is called Bastille Day, and it celebrates a revolution that happened in France in 1789. On Bastille Day, there are parades, speeches, and fireworks. French restaurants in other parts of the world often have special events on that day.

Fashion

French people are famous for making and wearing beautiful fabrics and clothes. For example, people in France came up with the idea of lace about 700 years ago.

High-heeled shoes were invented in France more than 400 years ago. In those days, men wore these shoes. Today, it's usually women who wear high heels.

Nineteenth-century French painting showing a boy wearing a lace collar

French high-heeled shoe from the 1600s

24

More than 300 years ago, people in France came up with the idea of wearing **neckties.** The first neckties were called *cravats.* The French also invented **suits.** The original suits were created more than 200 years ago. Back then, men often wore suits to ride horses. Today, both men and women often wear suits when they go to work.

Seventeenth-century French prince wearing high-heeled shoes

An early version of the necktie

French men wearing suits in the 1800s

25

A Recipe from France

Do you know the difference between a moose and a **mousse?** Both words are pronounced the same way, but they have very different meanings. A moose is a big animal with horns. You might not want to eat one of those. A mousse is a famous kind of French pudding. And you will probably love eating mousse—especially the kind made out of chocolate! You can make chocolate mousse yourself, with the help of an adult.

Chocolate Mousse

To start, you'll need the following ingredients:
6 ounces of semisweet chocolate chips
1/4 cup of water
1 egg
1/2 cup of heavy cream

1/2 teaspoon vanilla extract
You'll also need the following equipment:
- an electric blender
- measuring spoons
- a measuring cup
- a small saucepan
- a wooden spoon
- four glasses

You can do the first part of the recipe by yourself, with an adult watching.
1. Wash your hands.
2. Using the measuring cup, get 1/4 cup of water and pour it into a saucepan.
3. Pour 1/2 cup of heavy cream into the measuring cup.
4. Using the measuring spoons, get 1/2 teaspoon of vanilla and pour it into the measuring cup with the cream.

5. Break the egg and add carefully pour it into the measuring cup, making sure that no pieces of eggshell fall in. Set the measuring cup aside.

You'll need an adult to do the next part of the recipe, but you can help out by reading the instructions out loud.

Chocolate mousse topped with almond slivers

1. Put the saucepan of water onto the stove, and heat it until it comes to a boil.
2. Pour the boiling water into the blender.
3. Pour the chocolate chips into the blender.
4. Cover the blender and blend at high speed for 15 seconds.
5. Pour the contents of the measuring cup into the blender. Cover again and blend until well mixed.

Now you can work on the recipe by yourself again, with an adult watching.

1. Carefully pour the contents of the blender into the four glasses, making sure that each glass has about the same amount. You can use the wooden spoon to scrape the contents out of the blender.
2. Put the glasses into the refrigerator.
3. Chill the glasses into the refrigerator until the stuff inside is firm. Now you are ready to try chocolate mousse!

How do you say....?

Many people think that French is a very pretty language.
Try saying the following words and you'll see why!

English	French	How to pronounce it
good morning	bonjour	bohn JOOWR
goodbye	au revoir	ahr-VWAH
please	s'il vous plaît	see voo PLAY
thank you	merci	mehr-SEE
airplane	avion	ah-vee-OHN
bus	bus	bewss
cheese	fromage	froh-MAHJ
necktie	cravate	crah-VAHT
shoe	soulier	SOO-lee-ay
suit	complet	cawm-PLEH

To find out more

Here are some other resources to help you learn more about France:

Books

Arnold, Helen. **Postcards From: France.** Raintree/Steck-Vaughn, 1996.

Farris, Katherine (editor). **Let's Speak French: a First Book of Words.** Viking, 1993.

Haskins, James and Benson, Kathleen. **Count Your Way Through France.** Carolrhoda Books, 1996.

Norbrook, Dominique. **Getting to Know France.** Passport Books, 1989.

Stein, Richard Conrad. **Cities of the World: Paris**. Children's Press, 1997.

Organizations and Online Sites

Bastille Day
http://www.premier-ministre. gouv.fr/ENG/HIST/FETNAT.HTM
Find out about one of France's most important holidays.

France—CityNet
http://www.city.net/countries/ france/
Find out today's weather in France—and discover a great list of web links about the country.

French Government Tourist Office
444 Madison Ave.
16th Floor
New York, NY 10022-6903
http://www.francetourism.com/

Info France-USA for kids
http://www.info-france-usa. org/fkids.htm
A site especially for kids, developed by the French Embassy in Washington, D.C.

Map of France
http://www.lib.utexas.edu/Libs/ PCL/Map_collection/europe/ France.GIF
Check out this online map of Italy, provided by the University of Texas at Austin.

Paris pages: culture
http://www.paris.org/culture. html
Learn all about France's capital city.

29

Glossary

continent one of the major land areas of Earth

crescent something shaped like the curved shape of the moon in its first or last quarter

equipment supplies or tools needed for a special purpose

food processor a kitchen machine that can chop or grind various foods

parachute a device made out of fabric that allows people to fall slowly to Earth when they jump out of airplanes

pasteurization a process that makes milk and other drinks safer and less likely to spoil

photography the art of taking pictures with a camera

revolution the overthrow of a government by people ruled by this government

scuba a special kind of equipment that allows people to breathe air while swimming so that they can stay underwater for a long time

seaplane an airplane that can take off from and land on water

soufflé a puffy, baked dish made from egg yolks, beaten egg whites, and a flavoring (such as cheese, chocolate, or fruit)

Teflon a special coating that makes pots and pans easy to clean

Index

Look what doesn't come from France!

The French are famous for making beautiful-smelling perfumes, such as Chanel No. 5 and Shalimar. But **perfume** did not originally come from France. It was invented more than 5,000 years ago in the Middle East.

Meet the Author

Miles Harvey is the author of several books for young people. He lives in Chicago with his wife, Rengin, and daughter, Azize. This book is dedicated, with thanks, to Julia Rose Joffe White and her mom.